NEW ZEALAND PANORAMA

by Kowhai Publishing

New Zealand's treasure is its landscape. Within these small islands of the southern Pacific Ocean are scenic delights comparable to any in the world — the massive snow capped peaks of the Southern Alps or the symmetrical volcanic cones of the Central Plateau, the giant Kauris of Waipoua Forest or the dense rainforest of Westland, the arid highcountry tussockland of the McKenzie Basin or the rolling green pastures of Taranaki, the secluded golden bays of Abel Tasman National Park or the broad 90 Mile Beach of North Cape. The variety is unending — lakes and rivers, fiords and farmlands, all within easy reach of each other.

Towns and cities are often situated around magnificent natural harbours or on the banks of deeply flowing rivers. They are refreshingly unsophisticated, as are their inhabitants who offer a friendly welcome to their country of which they are justifiably proud. New Zealanders are happy for you to share their scenic treasures and participate in the marvellous range of activities they can provide. Try tramping the National Park walkways and the deep sea fishing in the Bay of Islands. Ski the mountain basins and jetboat down exciting river gorges. Enjoy New Zealand!

THE MAORI

Iew Zealand is a multi cultural society but
ne first New Zealanders were the migrant
Iaori. They were fierce tribal warriors with
ntimidating tattoo (moko).
'oday's Maoris are much friendlier than the
raditional haka *(below)* would indicate. In
Iaori communities life centres around the
narae, a place of assembly in front of the
neeting house, and of prime importance in
ne village complex. The Ohinemutu Meeting
Iouse, Rotorua *(right)* is a fine example of
ne intricacies of master carving.
Rotorua is a centre for learning the
ignficance of inherent beliefs and skills
ound within Maori culture. A model village
as been established at Whakarewarewa
'here performances of traditional songs and
oi dances *(left)* are held, along with
emonstrations of carving and weaving.

CITIES

Set around the magnificent Waitemata Harbour which opens to the Hauraki Gulf, Auckland *(above)* deserves its title "City of Sails". A quarter of the country's population live in this the largest and most metropolitan of New Zealand's cities.

Wellington *(top right)* is the capital and seat of New Zealand Government. Many leading companies have their head offices downtown, from where access to the hill suburb of Kelburn is by cablecar.

The first settlers in the South Island city of Christchurch *(right)* were English, as the meandering Avon river, Gothic architecture and superb trees reflect. The city wizard entertains daily in Cathedral Square.

Street names in Dunedin *(far right)* are evidence of a Scottish ancestry. A delightful University city, it is resolute that progress will not be affected by its southern isolation.

WELLINGTON CABLE CAR

COASTS

With approximately 6,400 kms of coast most New Zealanders are within easy reach of a beach. Holiday baches and camp sites are scattered along eastern and western coastlines. The beaches of the far north, where Matapouri Bay *(right)* is situated, entice holidaymakers with their sheltered golden bays and clear warm water.
At Punakaiki *(opposite)* on the west coast of the South island, limestone cliffs display 'pancake rock' formations resulting from the action of heavy rainfall and stormy seas driving in from the Tasman. Even further south at Moeraki *(above)* on the east coast is another natural phenomena. Huge spherical boulders weighing several tonnes lie in clusters along the lonely beach.

MOUNTAINS

New Zealand can be justly proud of its mountains. The largest in the North Island rise from a central plateau in the Tongariro National Park. Mounts Ngauruhoe, Ruapehu and Tongariro, though most often dormant, are classified as active volcanoes. Mt. Egmont *(left top)* is a symmetrically coned extinct volcano and the focal point of Taranaki.

The Southern Alps form a backbone virtually the length of the South Island. Mt. Cook is the highest peak in the country at 3,764m. Spectacular glaciers in Westland and Mt. Cook National Parks attract many visitors. It is possible to land on the glaciers and on the 29km Tasman Glacier *(left)* you can ski down to a location where the ski plane will pick you up for a return run.

Lake Tekapo *(above)* is glacial fed, hence its milky turquoise water which greatly enhances the barren beauty of the McKenzie Basin.

GEOTHERMAL

Along with Iceland and Yellow Stone National Park, U.S.A., the North Island of New Zealand is one of the noted geothermal regions of the world. Its active volcanic belt is centred around Lake Taupo and extends to the offshore White Island. Mt. Ngauruhoe *(right)* can often be seen belching steam and gas and on occasions ash and lava. Hot lakes and colourful silicon terraces are a feature of the Rotorua landscape. So too are fascinating pools of boiling mud *(right below)*. But perhaps the most famous attraction is Pohutu Geyser *(below)* at Whakarewarewa. On a good day he is known to "play" to a height of 30 metres.
With all this thermal activity the occasional earthquake experience in New Zealand is not unexpected.

FLOWERS

New Zealand's rapidly changing and varied terrain makes for an interesting native flora. Giant pohutukawa trees *(right)* which line much of the northern coast are in full bloom at Christmas and provide an attractive area of shade, with often a cushion of grass beneath to relieve the heat of the sand.
A feature of the Mount Cook National Park in summer is this alpine buttercup *(below)* commonly called the Mount Cook Lily. It is found throughout alpine regions of the South Island.
The spring flowering native Kowhai *(far right)* prefers a cool, temperate climate and is more prevalent on flat or gentle hill country. The ancient Maori planted his potatoes when the Kowhai burst into flower and tuis, bellbirds, wax-eyes and native pigeons eagerly seek its sweet nectar.

FORESTS

Before the interference of man two thirds of New Zealand was dense forest inhabited solely by birds. The remaining stands of bush, as it is colloquially termed, are protected wherever possible. The Kauri is the "King of the Forest". Te Matua Ngahere *(below)* is a magnificent speciman of the Waipoua Kauri Forest, Northland. His girth measures 16.1m and he stands 30m tall.
Beech forest *(left)* covers the eastern slopes of the mountain ranges, in distinct contrast to the rainforest on the west. This stand is on the shores of Lake Te Anau. Treeferns *(left below)* are found throughout New Zealand and are a highlight of our bush. Their Maori name is ponga and the lush pale foliage is supported by a long, porous trunk. The distinctive shape of the cabbage tree *(left top)* is seen in more open areas. Here it nicely frames the view of Mitre Peak on Milford Sound.

SCENERY

The grandeur and variety of the scenery is perhaps New Zealand's greatest commodity. These four pictures are all from the South Island.

Fox Glacier *(left)*, at 13kms, is the longer of two splendid glaciers in South Westland. It is hard to accept that this river of ice, set amongst some of the highest peaks of the Southern Alps, is actually moving.

Queenstown *(below)* is a popular holiday resort summer and winter. From the Skyline gondola the view is of township, Frankton and the Southern Arm of Lake Wakatipu, with the Remarkables range behind.

The Sutherland Falls *(below left)* are the third highest in the world and a feature of the Milford Track, reputably one of the most scenic walks in the world. It begins at the head of Lake Te Anau and ends when a launch collects you at Milford Sound *(right)* where massive peaks rise straight from the fiord's deep seabed, 2km below.

Mount Cook located in the South Island, is New Zealand's highest peak at 3764m. It is known to the Maori as Aorangi "the cloud piecer".

Pohutu Geyser 'plays' at Whakarewarewa in Rotorua, the centre of New Zealand's geothermal area.

Mitre Peak is the most dominant of the peaks which rise steeply from the clear waters of Milford Sound, Fiordland.

The gondola cableway to Bob's Peak gives a superb view of Queenstown and the Southern Arm of Lake Wakatipu. The Remarkable Range forms the background.

The haka is a Maori ceremonial posture dance performed by male warriors, here in traditional piu-piu (flax shirt).

Auckland is New Zealand's largest city. The Auckland Harbour Bridge connects the North Shore to the central city.

BIRDS

The absence of predators enabled several species of giant fightless birds to graze New Zealand's forest and pastures before the arrival of man. The Dinornis Maximus was the tallest bird ever to have lived, with a height of 3 to 4 metres. Only the huge eagle and one species of Moa remained when the Polynesian hunters arrived. Luckily our national symbol, the Kiwi *(above)* still survives, though being a shy nocturnal forest dweller you will probably only see him in a zoo. The Takahe *(far left)* was also thought to have perished until rediscovered in 1948 amongst the tussockland of Fiordland. The world's only remaining alpine parrot is the native Kea *(top left)* found near ski-fields and mountain huts. He is a cheeky scavenger that will nibble at anything, so be warned.
The NZ pigeon *(left)* is one of our many endemic forest birds. He is totally herbivorous and enjoys the nectar of the Kowhai flower.

WILD ANIMALS

New Zealand's only native land mammal is the bat. Polynesian migrants introduced dogs and rats and in 1769 Captain Cook released pigs into the forest to provide meat for future seafaring visitors. The Red Deer *(right)* was one of the many species brought by the white settlers. They thrived in the seclusion of the bush and today attract hunters as a trophy of quality.

The Tuatara (Sphenodon punctatus) *(above)*, is unique to New Zealand. It is the only survivor of the otherwise extinct order of 'beak-headed' reptiles. He is found on offshore islands where he lives in burrows and if 60cm in length, is probably a century old.

Captain Cook's journal spoke of large numbers of fur seals *(left)* basking on the Fiordland coastline. Immediately they were sought after and slaughtered for oil and their fine skins. They became protected animals about the turn of the 20th Century.

ARMING

Jntil recently farming was the main industry of New Zealand and its primary produce amb, wool, beef and dairy products eagerly ought in the United Kingdom. Competition rom the E.E.C. has created a need for new nd varied markets, plus a more profitable tilization of the land. Diversification from raditional dairy herds *(left)* and large umbers of sheep *(above)* has led to the ntroduction of deer and goat farming on uitable grazing land.

Aore intensive horticulture has developed in he warmer climates of Keri Keri, Hawkes Bay, Nelson and Marlborough where Kiwi ruit vines *(top right)*, orchards and vineyards *right)* are prevalent. With increased nternational exposure the products of these ndustries are gaining increasing respect.

ENERGY

New Zealand resisted the need for nuclear powered generators. It has abundant sources of water which can be harnessed for hydro-powered electricity.
The lakes and rivers of the South Island are the main supply. Roxburgh Dam *(left)* is on the Clutha River, the largest water flow in New Zealand where even larger dams are being built to utilize this natural asset.
Geothermal power offers an interesting alternative energy source. Steam feeds the electric turbine generators in the power houses at Wairakei *(top left)*, on the banks of the Waikato River.
Exciting hydrocarbon finds give hope for a future not totally reliant on the importing of oil. Natural gas and oil are being successfully drilled at Kapuni *(above)* and at several offshore fields, principally located near Taranaki.

SPORT

Sport has been referred to as a national religion. This may be true but it definitely is not just "rugby, racing and beer", although our All Blacks did win the World Rugby Cup in 1987 and our thoroughbred yearling sales do attract leading world buyers.

It is natural for a New Zealander to lead an active life. From an early age our children are encouraged to participate in a variety of team and individual sports. Our yachtsmen, canoeists, equestrians, squash and triathalon athletes have gained top international reputations. But at grass root level the emphasis on all sport in New Zealand is participation.

(top right) Yacht race on Auckland's Waitemata Harbour.
(right) Racing at Riccarton during the Grand National meeting.
(far right) Provincial rugby teams Canterbury and Wellington compete for the Ranfurly Shield.
(above) Saturday cricket at Hagley Park, Christchurch.

2202
2244
3449

DRC

CLUB

LEISURE

There is a fine line between sport and leisure activities in New Zealand. Activity is the key word. With wide open spaces New Zealanders enjoy the outdoor life.
Tramping is popular, especially in many National Parks found in both Islands. This group *(below)*, is heading toward Fiordland from the head of Lake Wakatipu, an area noted for scenic walks and good fishing. Mountaineering, crosscountry and heli-skiing are for the more daring. There are numerous commercial and club ski-fields available to acquire the necessary skills.
Rural areas often have an annual Sports Day. Tuatapere, in Southland *(opposite)*, have theirs on New Years Day. It is a day of woodchopping and sawing, Highland dancing, athletics and cycling — fun for everyone.

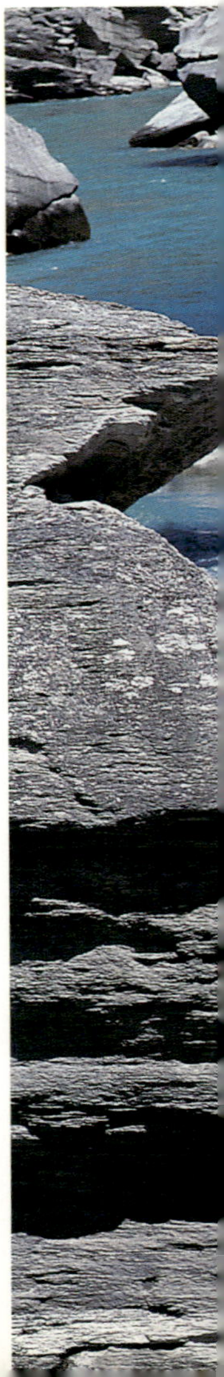

ACTION

The "Kiwi" has an adventurous nature, perhaps that is why rafting has become so popular. There is certainly enough "white water" in rivers of both islands which is graded from 1 to 5 according to the ability (and nerve) needed. This raft *(top right)* is negotiating the rapids of the Tongariro River near Taupo.
The jet boat was designed by a New Zealander, C.W. Hamilton, for the shallow braided rivers of Canterbury. It has however been found suitable for most conditions, including the narrow gorges of the Shotover River outside Queenstown *(right)*.
The stalking and landing of huge brown and rainbow trout that frequent the New Zealand rivers and lakes makes for a more peaceful, while still exciting pastime.
Uncountable other activities go on around the country, with large numbers of enthusiastic participants — surf carnivals, fun runs, coast to coast triathalons. New Zealanders are people of action.

SHOTOVER JET

COTTAGE
Adults
Children 20